P9-BYE-166

J
323.1
CRE

Crewe, Sabrina

The 1963 civil rights
march

The 1963 Civil Rights March

Sabrina Crewe and Scott Ingram

Gareth Stevens Publishing

A WORLD ALMANAC EDUCATION GROUP COMPANY

Please visit our web site at: www.garethstevens.com
For a free color catalog describing Gareth Stevens Publishing's list of high-quality books and multimedia programs, call 1-800-542-2595 (USA) or 1-800-387-3178 (Canada). Gareth Stevens Publishing's fax: (414) 332-3567.

Library of Congress Cataloging-in-Publication Data

Crewe, Sabrina.
   The 1963 civil rights march / by Sabrina Crewe and Scott Ingram.
     p. cm. — (Events that shaped America)
   Includes bibliographical references and index.
   ISBN 0-8368-3411-9 (lib. bdg.)
   1. March on Washington for Jobs and Freedom, Washington, D.C., 1963—
Juvenile literature. 2. Civil rights demonstrations—Washington (D.C.)—History—
20th century—Juvenile literature. 3. African Americans—Civil rights—History—
20th century—Juvenile literature. I. Ingram, Scott. II. Title. III. Series.
   F200.C74   2005
   323.1196'073'009046—dc22   2004058184

This North American edition first published in 2005 by
Gareth Stevens Publishing
A WRC Media Company
330 West Olive Street, Suite 100
Milwaukee, WI 53212 USA

Produced by Discovery Books
Editor: Sabrina Crewe
Designer and page production: Sabine Beaupré
Photo researcher: Sabrina Crewe
Maps and diagrams: Stefan Chabluk
Gareth Stevens editorial direction: Mark J. Sachner
Gareth Stevens editor: Monica Rausch
Gareth Stevens art direction: Tammy West
Gareth Stevens production: Jessica Morris

Photo credits: Corbis: cover, pp. 4, 5, 7, 8, 9, 12, 13, 18, 19, 20, 21, 22, 23, 26, 27;
Library of Congress: pp. 6, 10, 11, 14, 15, 16, 24, 25.

Printed in the United States of America

1 2 3 4 5 6 7 8 9 09 08 07 06 05

Contents

Introduction

Thousands of marchers assembled at the Washington Monument (in the background in this photo). Then they marched to the Lincoln Memorial about 1 mile (1.6 kilometers) away.

A Gentle Army

"No one could remember an invading army quite as gentle as the two hundred thousand civil-rights marchers who occupied Washington today. . . . The sweetness and patience of the crowd may have set some sort of national high-water mark in mass decency."

Russell Baker, describing the 1963 march, the New York Times

The March on Washington

On Wednesday, August 28, 1963, more than 200,000 Americans from around the country came to Washington, D.C. They were there to take part in the March on Washington for Jobs and Freedom. After gathering in the center of the city, the marchers listened to speeches. One of the speakers was Martin Luther King, Jr., who gave a speech that has become one of the most famous in U.S. history.

The 1963 March on Washington was a protest about **civil rights**. It was also the

4

The Goals of the March

The organizers of the March on Washington had several goals. The first was to ask Congress to pass a new civil rights law. The law would end **discrimination** in housing, employment, and education and protect voting rights. The second goal of the march was to demand that the government start a huge program to help all workers get jobs, whatever their race. In addition, the marchers wanted a **minimum wage** of $2 an hour for all workers. They also wanted the government to protect people's rights under the U.S. Constitution.

There were so many people at the March on Washington that the crowd stretched back from the Lincoln Memorial as far as the eye could see.

largest political **demonstration** that had been held up to that point. It is remembered today as one of the most powerful, peaceful protests ever staged in the nation's capital.

The Civil Rights Movement

The event took place a hundred years after President Abraham Lincoln issued the **Emancipation** Proclamation, freeing slaves in the South. One hundred years had passed, but racial inequality was still present in U.S. society. The march was part of the civil rights movement, a struggle by black people to achieve the basic rights that are promised to all Americans in the **Constitution**.

Chapter One

The Struggle for Civil Rights

Free but Not Equal

For about 250 years, African and African-American slaves were bought and sold in North America. In 1865, however, the Thirteenth **Amendment** banned slavery throughout the United States. African Americans were free, but they were far from equal with whites. Their inequality was especially noticeable in the South, where most blacks lived.

Travel on the Railroad in a "Free" Country

"I have traveled in this free country for twenty hours without anything to eat; not because I had no money to pay for it, but because I was colored. Other passengers of a lighter hue had breakfast, dinner and supper. In traveling we are thrown in 'Jim Crow' cars, denied the privilege of buying a berth in the sleeping coach."

B. W. Arnett, "The Black Laws," 1886

Like other public facilities in the South, these water fountains at the county courthouse in Albany, Georgia, were segregated. Segregated didn't just mean separate —it meant better facilities for whites.

Segregation Takes Hold

It was **segregation** that kept blacks from gaining equality. State laws in the South, known as **Jim Crow** laws, made sure that blacks and whites went to separate schools, used separate public facilities, ate in separate restaurants, stayed in separate hotels, and more. Local governments also passed laws that made it impossible for African Americans to vote in elections, even though they were U.S. citizens.

By the beginning of the twentieth century, southern states had two separate societies: black and white. Segregation spread widely across the South and into other states.

Control by Terror

Whites controlled blacks not just with segregation, but with violence. White Southerners formed organizations such as the Ku Klux Klan, which used violence and threats against blacks. The brutality increased during the 1920s and 1930s when the Ku Klux Klan grew to over two million members and spread to the Midwest. **Lynching** became one of the most common forms of terror used by the Ku Klux Klan.

Jim Crow Everywhere
"If there must be Jim Crow cars on railroads . . . there should be Jim Crow [seats] on passenger boats . . . there should be Jim Crow waiting [rooms] at all stations, and Jim Crow eating houses."

From a South Carolina newspaper, ridiculing segregation with examples that later became true, 1881

These World War II pilots were all trained at the Tuskegee Institute for African Americans in Alabama. Because of the Tuskegee pilots' bravery and skill, many white Americans acquired a new respect for blacks in the 1940s.

A Question of Equality

"We come then to the question presented: Does segregation of children in public schools solely on the basis of race, even though the physical facilities and other 'tangible' factors may be equal, deprive the children of the minority group of equal educational opportunities? We believe that it does."

From the Supreme Court Brown v. Board of Education *decision, 1954*

The NAACP and the New Deal

Black Americans, together with some whites who supported their cause, eventually formed a national organization to fight segregation. This group, formed in 1909, was the National Association for the Advancement of Colored People (NAACP). Over the years, the NAACP tried to get Congress to pass laws that would end racial violence and give blacks equal rights.

When Franklin D. Roosevelt became president in 1933, his New Deal programs created government-funded jobs for working Americans. The NAACP pushed for the inclusion of black people in the employment programs and encouraged Roosevelt to help African Americans in other ways.

Resistance to Integration

In the 1940s, progress was made as African Americans successfully fought discrimination. In 1947, for instance, Jackie Robinson became the first African American to play major league baseball. In 1948, President Harry S. Truman desegregated the U.S. military forces.

In the South, however, whites would not accept blacks as their equals. Many white southern officials refused to obey a 1954 U.S. **Supreme Court** decision to end segregation in schools. In spite of the court's order, under 2 percent of black children in the South attended white schools. The conflict over desegregating education continued into the 1960s.

Little Rock Central High School

In 1957, the school board in Little Rock, Arkansas, attempted to **integrate** its high school. Governor Orval Faubus, who believed in segregation, sent in the Arkansas National Guard to keep out black students. President Dwight D. Eisenhower responded by sending about one thousand U.S. Army soldiers to Little Rock to escort the black children to school.

Black students guarded by soldiers walk up the steps of Little Rock Central High in Arkansas in 1957.

In 1956, after the Montgomery bus boycott had ended successfully, Martin Luther King, Jr., (second row, left) took a ride on a Montgomery bus sitting next to a white man.

The Montgomery Bus Boycott

In the South, public transportation was segregated by law. In 1955, Rosa Parks, an active NAACP member in Montgomery, Alabama, refused to surrender her seat on a city bus to a white man and move to the rear, "colored" section. She was arrested for her refusal.

In protest, the black community in Montgomery **boycotted** the city buses. Thousands of African Americans walked miles to work each day or organized carpools. The white officials and citizens were angry, but Montgomery's black community held out for 381 days. In late 1956, the U.S. Supreme Court prohibited segregation on buses, and the boycott ended. Meanwhile, the dignity and determinaton of the people of Montgomery had attracted the attention of the world.

A New Leader Emerges

Martin Luther King, Jr., a twenty-six-year-old local minister, had been spokesperson for the boycotters. Afterward, he joined other civil rights leaders to create the Southern

Christian Leadership Conference (SCLC) in 1957. The SCLC became the main organization for church-based, nonviolent, protest groups across the South.

Nonviolent Protest

King was an admirer of Mahatma Gandhi, who had led the people of India through many years of nonviolent action to achieve independence from British rule. The early civil rights **activists** in the United States, like King, wanted to achieve equality through peaceful determination as Gandhi had done.

In the early 1960s, nonviolent protests became the main tool of the civil rights movement to achieve integration. One kind of protest was a sit-in, at which people would sit in a place and refuse to move. African Americans and whites would sit-in together at restaurants, theaters, and other public places that were segregated or for "whites only." Another nonviolent protest was made by "freedom riders." These young people rode interstate buses to cities in the South and defied segregation rules for passengers on the buses.

The first sit-in, shown here, was at a lunch counter in Greensboro, North Carolina. The first protestors were soon joined by many more, both black and white.

Marching in Birmingham

In April and May 1963, the SCLC organized marchers to demonstrate in downtown Birmingham, Alabama, to protest segregation. No city was more hostile to integration than Birmingham. By the beginning of May, there were over two thousand marchers in jail. The police did everything within their powers to stop the protests. Violence came to a head when officers turned fire hoses on marchers, including children, and went after them with dogs. Nightly news broadcasts of the assault on peaceful protestors shocked the nation and the world.

June 1963

The sit-ins, marches, and freedom rides had gained the attention of President John F. Kennedy. Kennedy did not want to upset white Southerners in Congress because he needed their political support. Events in June 1963, however, forced Kennedy to take action to support integration.

This photo shows a scene from the 1963 protests in Brimingham. The force of water from hoses used by police was powerful enough to slam some protestors against walls. Other people were injured by police dogs.

On June 11, 1963, Alabama's governor, George Wallace, personally blocked the door to the University of Alabama to prevent black students from registering. In response, Kennedy authorized **federal** troops to force Wallace to step aside.

The next evening, June 12, Kennedy said that Americans could no longer ask black citizens to "be content with . . . patience and delay." He urged Congress to act on civil rights.

Hours later, Medgar Evers, the leading NAACP official in Mississippi, was assassinated. The funeral of Evers, a World War II veteran and a strong voice for civil rights, drew political leaders from across the nation.

Kennedy Demands New Legislation

One week after Evers' death, Kennedy requested specific **legislation** from Congress. He said it needed to ban segregation in public facilities, strengthen the laws enforcing school integration, and offer greater federal protection of voting rights. Within weeks, Kennedy's bill became the focus for the biggest peaceful demonstration the nation had ever seen.

Segregation Forever
"I say segregation now . . . segregation tomorrow . . . segregation forever!"

George Wallace, inaugural address as governor of Alabama, 1963

Chapter Two

Planning the March

Making the Decision

In the winter of 1962 to 1963, civil rights leaders had begun discussing a mass demonstration in support of their cause. It was the idea of A. Philip Randolph, a civil rights leader who fought for employment rights for African Americans.

The Big Six

Asa Philip Randolph (1889–1979) was director of the March on Washington. He and the other march leaders were known as the "Big Six." **Martin Luther King, Jr.,** (1929–1968) of the SCLC was the most famous civil rights leader of the 1960s. **Roy Wilkins** (1901–1981) led the NAACP from 1931 to 1977. **James Farmer** (1920–1999) was cofounder of the Congress of Racial Equality (CORE), which organized the freedom rides. **John Lewis** (born 1940) was a former freedom rider and president of the Student Nonviolent Coordinating Committee (SNCC), a group that grew out of the sit-in protests. **Whitney Young** (1921–1971) was director of the National Urban League, an organization that protected the civil rights of minority groups.

The Big Six (from left to right): John Lewis, Whitney Young, A. Philip Randolph, Martin Luther King, Jr., James Farmer, and Roy Wilkins.

By June 1963, Martin Luther King and the SCLC had agreed to work with Randolph toward a march in the summer of that year. The leader of the NAACP, Roy Wilkins, then pledged his support. In addition, white church and labor organizations offered their help.

On June 11, King announced plans to the media for a demonstration in Washington, D.C. In early July, the march date was set for August 28, 1963. The event was named the "March on Washington for Jobs and Freedom."

The Organizer

The march had six leaders, important civil rights workers whose involvement attracted people to come to the march. Behind the scenes, the organization was done by Bayard Rustin. He was known to be a brilliant organizer of civil rights protests, such as the Montgomery bus boycott.

When the final decision to hold the march was made on July 2, Rustin had less than two months to organize the enormous event. Working day and night, he accomplished an amazing amount. Within two weeks, he had printed and sent out two thousand copies of his Organizing Manual to civil rights offices across the nation to help each local group prepare.

Bayard Rustin planned all the details of the march, from the schedule of events to the efficient movement of huge numbers of people. Here, he explains a map to a group of marshals, whose job it would be to keep order among the marchers.

AS IN THE HEARTS OF THE PEOPLE
FOR WHOM HE SAVED THE UNION
THE MEMORY OF ABRAHAM LINCOLN
IS ENSHRINED FOREVER

Raising Money

Although civil rights organizations had pledged money for the event, thousands of dollars still had to be raised. Rustin raised funds by selling march buttons for 25¢ apiece. By early August, more than 175,000 had been sold and 150,000 more were ordered.

Cooperation

President Kennedy, who had at first been doubtful about the march, gave his support to the idea. This official approval led to a unique cooperation. Both the march organizers and the government were determined to keep the protest nonviolent. Their common purpose meant that the organizers worked closely with government officials, the police, and the city authorities in Washington, D.C.

Being Prepared

The organizers and authorities took steps to ensure peace and order. All police officers in the city had their vacations

The march was set to start at the Washington Monument, which stands south of the White House in a large open part of the area known as the Mall. After opening ceremonies there, marchers would walk west down either of two routes, Constitution Avenue or Independence Avenue, for about 1 mile (1.6 km). They would assemble again at the steps of the Lincoln Memorial, a symbol of freedom to all African Americans, to listen to the main speeches.

canceled for the day. The National Guard was called in, as well as local police reserve units and firefighters. The president's administration added its security forces to help, and the march organizers enlisted hundreds of volunteers to act as marshals. Meanwhile, U.S. Attorney General Robert Kennedy, the president's brother, ordered police dogs to be kept completely away from the marchers.

The Justice Department and the police worked with the march organizers on planning the route. Government workers also helped develop the most modern public address system possible, to allow all the participants to hear the broadcast speeches and messages.

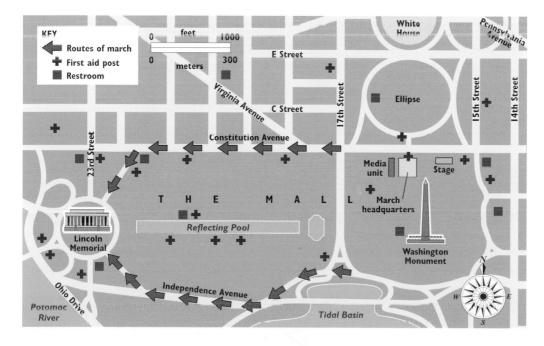

This map shows the area of the march and the official routes that protestors would take from the Washington Monument to the Lincoln Memorial.

Chapter Three

The March on Washington

Marchers arrive at Union Station in Washington, D.C., on the morning of August 28.

Arriving in Washington

On August 28, 1963, more than 200,000 Americans poured into Washington, D.C. Many had left their homes weeks earlier. Members of one New York City chapter of CORE walked the 230 miles (370 km) to the capital in thirteen days. A group of college students arrived after weeks of walking and hitchhiking 700 miles (1,126 km) from their college in Alabama.

Trains and buses pulled into Washington's Union Station shortly after dawn. Many of the buses had been organized by local branches of the NAACP, SCLC, and other groups to

Constant Harassment

"We were constantly harassed. People shouting obscenities, telling us where to go . . . people who didn't agree with what we were doing."

Joy Bauer, a college student who traveled to the march from Florida

transport people to Washington, D.C., from their communities. Thousands of people traveled in these buses. In addition to the regular trains arriving at the station, an extra twenty-one trains were specially arranged and brought more than thirty thousand marchers.

A Huge Crowd

It was late summer in Washington, D.C., and the weather was hot and humid. Usually the capital appeared empty at that time of year, but on August 28, 1963, it was very different.

In the morning, thousands upon thousands of people assembled on the slope beside the Washington Monument to wait for the march to begin. The crowd was mostly black, but there were thousands of whites as well. Some marchers were wealthy and famous, but most were ordinary working people.

When the Sun Came Up
"Somewhere between Baltimore and D.C. the sun began to come up. When you are in a bus like this at night, you are in a closed world. You can't see what is around you. As the sun came up you see the whole freeway. All lanes completely jammed with buses. That's the moment we knew this march would be a big success."

Bruce Hartford, a student who took a bus from Connecticut, describing his journey to Washington, D.C.

With the Capitol building in the background, a stream of marchers heads to the Washington Monument for the first gathering.

Gathering at the Washington Monument

At the Washington Monument, the organizers had set up a stage for the morning's entertainment. There, black and white performers sang songs that focused on the themes of the civil rights movement.

The March Begins

Although the march did not start officially until noon, thousands of people started walking shortly after 11:00 A.M. When the march leaders heard that the event had begun without them, they rushed from a meeting at the Capitol to join the crowd. Then the march started officially, and a great tide of people headed toward the Lincoln Memorial.

Thousands of Signs

Many people carried the red, white, and blue signs that had been made by the march organizers. The signs carried messages that addressed issues from labor to justice to civil rights. Other marchers brought their own signs. Hundreds of marchers from the United Auto Workers **union** (UAW) carried mass-produced signs such as, "UAW Says Jobs and Freedom for Every American." Some people had handmade signs. A young marcher carried a sign that read, "There Would Be More of Us Here But So Many of Us Are in Jail. Freedom Now." A woman carried a sign that demanded, "We Must Be Accorded Full Rights as Americans Not in the Future but Now."

At the march headquarters, volunteers prepare signs to give to protestors.

At the Lincoln Memorial

By mid-morning, the temperature neared 90° F (32° C) and humid air hung like a blanket over the city. By 2:00 P.M., all of the marchers had reached the Lincoln Memorial or the Reflecting Pool in front of it. The event began with the national anthem and an opening prayer delivered by a Washington, D.C., Catholic leader.

Speeches, Prayers, and Songs

Philip Randolph then delivered the first speech of the afternoon. Soon after, Bayard Rustin gave a "Tribute to Negro Women Fighters for Freedom." Although no women spoke at the event, Rustin introduced six women, including Rosa Parks, who had been important in civil rights.

As the sweltering afternoon wore on, march leaders John Lewis, James Farmer, Whitney Young, and Roy Wilkins spoke. Between speeches, there were prayers and music. A performance by famous gospel singer, Mahalia Jackson, brought the crowd to its feet, cheering and whistling.

As temperatures rose, some demonstrators plunged their feet into the Reflecting Pool. The atmosphere at the march was friendly and peaceful.

King's Speech

In the late afternoon, as the scorching sun at last began to sink in the sky, Martin Luther King stepped to the microphone to begin his speech. King began, "I am happy to join with you today in what will go down in history as the greatest demonstration for freedom in the history of our nation." King praised Lincoln's role in ending slavery but said that black people remained slaves to discrimination. He declared it was time to change.

King spoke of his dream for a better future. He said, "I have a dream my four little children will one day live in a nation where they will not be judged by the color of their skin but by the content of their character."

The crowd thundered its approval as King concluded: "When we allow freedom to ring, when we let it ring from every village and every hamlet, from every state and every city, we will be able to speed up that day when all God's children, black men and white men, Jews and Gentiles, Protestants and Catholics, will be able to join hands and sing in the words of the old Negro spiritual: 'Free at last! Free at last! Thank God Almighty, we are free at last!'"

The End of the March

The rally was coming to an end. Rustin read out the goals of the march. His words were followed by a short prayer, and the crowd departed quickly and without incident. A cleanup

squad of several hundred volunteers organized by Rustin
made sure that every scrap of litter was picked up. As evening
descended in the Mall, it was hard to imagine that more than
200,000 people had so recently filled the area.

Greatest Day
"I went back to
the grounds
about six or
seven o'clock that
evening. There
was nothing but
the wind blowing
across the
reflection pool,
moving and
blowing and
keeping music.
We were so
proud that no
violence had
taken place that
day. We were so
pleased. . . . This
was the greatest
day of my life."

*Ralph Abernathy,
civil rights
activist,* Voices
of Freedom *by
Henry Hampton
and Steve Fayer,
1990*

Abraham Lincoln's statue sits inside the Lincoln Memorial.

23

Chapter Four

After the March

A photo by James Kerales shows an important march that took place in Alabama in 1965. Protestors walked from Selma to Montgomery to demand a law to protect voting rights.

The Civil Rights Act of 1964

Less than three months after the March on Washington, President Kennedy was assassinated, and Vice President Lyndon B. Johnson took office. In a speech to Congress, Johnson called for lawmakers to pass the Civil Rights Act to honor the fallen president.

The act was passed on July 2, 1964. It outlawed racial discrimination in facilities such as hotels, amusement parks, and other public places. It aimed to protect voting rights and insure equal opportunities in employment. Finally, it gave the U.S. attorney general the power to desegregate schools.

> ### Enough Talking
> "We have talked long enough in this country. We have talked for one hundred years or more. It is now time to write the next chapter—and to write it in the books of law."
>
> *President Lyndon B. Johnson, speech to Congress, November 27, 1963*

King Is Assassinated

In spite of the new law, many people continued to live with discrimination. Anger about lack of jobs and poor housing caused race riots to flare in cities across the country in the mid-1960s.

Then, on April 4, 1968, Martin Luther King was assassinated in Memphis, Tennessee. He was thirty-nine years old. After the death of the much-loved civil rights leader, the peaceful side of the civil rights movement appeared to lose its energy. Protestors found other ways of expressing their discontent.

"Today you have a new generation of black people who have come on the scene, who have become disenchanted with the entire system, who have become disillusioned over the system, and who are ready now and willing to do something about it."
— Malcolm X —

The militant movement that grew in the mid-1960s was called "Black Power." Malcolm X (above, center right) was a Black Power leader.

The Civil Rights Movement Changes

Young African Americans increasingly turned to **militant** organizations such as the Nation of Islam and the Black Panther Party. These militant groups thought the nonviolent movement was too moderate. Black leaders such as Malcolm X, Huey Newton, and Stokely Carmichael called for violent resistance to racial prejudice and brutality.

The new leaders also appealed to African Americans to take pride in their history and heritage. They discarded the terms "Negro" and "colored" and used the terms "black" and "African American." They said blacks should separate from whites instead of trying to integrate.

Conclusion

A Beginning
"1963 is not an end, but a beginning."

Martin Luther King, Jr.

The March Remembered

Many people see the March on Washington as a special moment in the history of race relations in the United States. For them, it was the highest achievement of the nonviolent civil rights movement of the early 1960s.

Today, the march is generally remembered for King's dramatic speech. The two men who organized the march—Philip Randolph and Bayard Rustin—are often overlooked. It was because of their amazing efforts, however, that such a huge event was put together in a period of less than two months. As it turned out, it was one of the best-organized and most peaceful demonstrations of its size ever held.

President George W. Bush lays a wreath at King's grave on Martin Luther King Day in January 2004. Coretta Scott King, the widow of the civil rights leader, watches.

26

Achievements and Challenges

Martin Luther King Day in January, when the civil rights leader is honored on the Monday nearest his birthday, has been declared a federal holiday. The struggles and legislation of the 1960s, together with later policies of **affirmative action**, have produced results. There are now record numbers of black elected officials around the country, and educational achievement among African Americans has improved.

Poverty, however, remains an enemy of minorities in the United States. Not only African Americans, but Hispanics and other ethnic groups continue to earn less and hold fewer jobs of influence than white Americans. In spite of King's dream, the nation is still separated in this way.

A Memorial in Washington, D.C.

In the summer of 2003, on the fortieth anniversary of the event, a memorial plaque was dedicated to the 1963 March on Washington at the Lincoln Memorial. Among those in attendance was Coretta Scott King, the widow of Martin Luther King. Also in attendance was the only surviving speaker from the 1963 march, John Lewis. Forty years on, the young leader of the SNCC had become a congressional representative from his home state of Georgia in the heart of the once-segregated South.

Time Line

1863   President Abraham Lincoln issues Emancipation Proclamation.

1865   Thirteenth Amendment is enacted.

1909   National Association for the Advancement of Colored People is founded.

1947   Jackie Robinson becomes first black major league baseball player.

1948   President Harry S. Truman desegregates U.S. military forces.

1954   U.S. Supreme Court outlaws school segregation.

1955   Montgomery bus boycott begins.

1956   U.S. Supreme Court outlaws segregation on buses.

1957   President Dwight D. Eisenhower sends federal troops to ensure school integration in Little Rock, Arkansas.

1960   Sit-in protests begin.
Student Nonviolent Coordinating Committee is founded.

1961   Freedom rides begin.

1962   President John F. Kennedy sends federal troops to the University of Mississippi to ensure integration.
U.S. Supreme Court outlaws segregation on all forms of public transportation.

1963   May: Police use fire hoses and dogs to attack civil rights marchers in Birmingham, Alabama.
June 11: Alabama governor George Wallace attempts to block registration by black students at the University of Alabama.
June 12: Mississippi civil rights leader Medgar Evers is murdered.
June 19: Kennedy requests civil rights legislation from Congress.
August 28: March on Washington for Jobs and Freedom.
November 22: Kennedy is assassinated.

1964   July 2: Civil Rights Act of 1964 is signed.

1968   April 4: Martin Luther King, Jr., is assassinated.

Things to Think About and Do

Living with Segregation

Find out more about what it was like to live in the South under segregation during the first half of the 1900s. Imagine that you are growing up in a segregated society, and think about what it would feel like not to have the basic rights, freedoms, and opportunities that you have today.

Marching on Washingtton

Pretend that your family has come to Washington, D.C., to take part in the 1963 March on Washington. Describe your day: the journey to Washington, the events that took place, the people you met, and the things you saw.

Glossary

activist: person who takes action to support or protest issues.

affirmative action: action taken to improve opportunities for minorities.

Amendment: official change or addition to the U.S. Constitution.

boycott: refuse to do business with a particular company in protest at its policies.

civil rights: basic rights—such as voting and education—of every person.

constitution: basic rules of government for a nation.

demonstration: public show of beliefs or feelings by a group of people in support of a cause.

discrimination: showing preference for one group over another; in the case of racial discrimination before the civil rights movement, white people were treated better than black people.

emancipation: freeing of people, especially enslaved African Americans.

federal : having to do with the whole nation or with national government.

integrate: get rid of segregation; the same as desegregate.

Jim Crow: fictional character of the 1800s created by a white performer to make fun of black people. The name was used for the segregation laws of the 1800s and 1900s.

legislation: process of making laws; and the laws that are made.

lynch: use a group of people unlawfully to attack and kill a victim.

militant: using aggression and sometimes violence in protesting a cause.

minimum wage: least amount of money a person must be paid for working.

segregation: separation of people of different races.

Supreme Court: highest court in the United States, which has the power to make final decisions on matters of law and the Constitution.

union: organization that campaigns and negotiates for better working conditions for its members, who are usually workers from a particular trade or type of business.

Further Information

Books

Alcorn, Stephen. *Let It Shine: Stories of Black Women Freedom Fighters.* Gulliver, 2000.

Ditchfield, Christin. *Knowing Your Civil Rights* (True Books). Children's Press, 2004.

Hatt, Christine. *Martin Luther King, Jr.* (Judge for Yourself). World Almanac, 2004.

Parks, Rosa. *Dear Mrs. Parks: A Dialogue with Today's Youth.* Lee and Low, 1997.

Summer L. S. *The March on Washington* (Journey to Freedom). Child's World, 2001.

Web Sites

www.civilrightsmuseum.org/gallery/movement.asp National Civil Rights Museum has online exhibitions about the struggle for civil rights since the time of slavery.

www.naacp.org Web site of the National Association for the Advancement of Colored People offers historical information and current news about African-American civil rights.

www.usinfo.state.gov/usa/civilrights Department of State web site honors the fortieth anniversary of the March on Washington with photographs, articles, documents, and many good links.

Useful Addresses

National Association for the Advancement of Colored People
4805 Mt. Hope Drive
Baltimore, MD 21215
Telephone: (410) 521-4939

Index